Depression & Pregnancy:
31 Useful Tips To Manage Depression During & After Pregnancy

By Sophie Acker

Contents

Introduction.

Even though pregnancy can be a wonderful time filled with hope and expectations for the expectant mother, with the normal ebb and flow of hormones and the rollercoaster ride of emotions, it can be difficult to stay on an even keel (just ask the expecting father!). Sadly, this can be compounded when depression arises during pregnancy.

Statistics from the American Psychological Association indicate that approximately one in five women experience some depression during pregnancy, a fact that can seem startling when you consider how joyful those nine months are supposed to be.1 The depression may be transient and less severe in most, but according to those same statistics, 10 percent of pregnant women experience serious clinical depression.

Clinical depression can profoundly impact not only the mother, but the fetus as well. For instance, mothers who are depressed during pregnancy often give birth to infants with noticeably lower birth weights. Therefore, if you or someone you love is pregnant, it is important to recognize the symptoms of depression and to discuss them with your medical provider.

Signs that depression might be a problem during a pregnancy are relatively easy to spot..

---

[1] Identifying and treating Maternal depression: strategies & Considerations for HealtH plans
nIHCM foundation Issue Brief June 2010

You might find yourself fatigued constantly (beyond normal pregnancy tiredness) or having difficulty sleeping. You or someone you love might notice that your attention to personal needs, whether it's hygiene or pregnancy fitness and diet has dissipated. Or perhaps you find yourself ambivalent about giving birth – not frightened or excited, but simply willing to do it, because it will happen regardless. It is important if you notice these symptoms or if someone comes to you with concern, that you discuss this with your OB-GYN, midwife, doula or a therapist.

While the majority of pregnant women do not suffer from depression during those glowing nine months, there is a period of "baby blues," which is a normal reaction after giving birth. However, approximately nine to 16 percent of women develop post-partum depression, which lingers and can impact the new mother and her ability to care for her infant.

Let's take a closer look at depression during pregnancy and see how it can be handled so that with help, you can enjoy the wonderful miracle and experience of your child growing and moving within your womb

As mentioned previously, 10-20 percent of pregnant women develop prenatal depression. This can greatly affect sleep habits, appetite, self-esteem, interest in activities, (particularly with activities previously enjoyed), and can bring on serious bouts of crying as well as a lack of attachment to the baby.

Several prenatal studies done on pregnant women indicated that the presence of raised cortisol levels at 20 weeks of gestation coincides with prenatal depression. Raised cortisol levels during pregnancy greatly increase the risk of premature birth, low-birth weight and behavioral problems as the child grows.[2]

The cortisol levels in these studies were then surprisingly associated with low serotonin and low dopamine levels in the mother (both serotonin and dopamine contribute to positive moods in people). Those indicators point to a less than ideal pregnancy and need to be addressed for the sake of both mother and child.

Caffeine intake and/or drug abuse also compound prenatal depression. The ingestion of caffeine has been known to increase a person's cortisol levels significantly and that is especially true during pregnancy. Of course, this directly impacts the baby.

Other issues contribute to prenatal depression, such as the young age of the mother, lack of education, socio-economic issues and the lack of a supportive partner during pregnancy.[3] Feelings of being overwhelmed can develop quickly and spiral out of control as the pregnancy goes on and the mother's feelings are not addressed. Genetics can also play a key role in a woman's susceptibility to depression.

Infants whose mothers were depressed in pregnancy are shown to be not as active as infants of non-depressed mothers.

---

[2] ibid
[3] ibid

3

As the child grows, acting out or other disturbances may present themselves. Studies have shown that even through teenage years, the child himself may be prone to depression. This can play havoc on the child and his/her behavior, often thwarting academic achievement and maturity.

Fortunately, in the past 15 years, the media has investigated and brought to light prenatal depression and its many facets. As a result, much more is known about this condition and how to combat it. We'll look at the positive treatments that are available a little later.

Now let's look at baby blues. It is a common occurrence following birth, one that impacts as much as 80 percent of all new mothers. If we consider all that happens within a woman's body, her emotions, the highs and lows, the everyday stressors in those formidable nine months and then the enormous build-up, which gives way to a life-changing event that, let's face it, ends with a squalling newborn who can't convey his needs other than through crying, it is not surprising that the blues develop. Normally, the baby blues appear within the first week after giving birth.

Signs that post-partum depression have developed in the mother can include spontaneous and frequent bouts of crying, sleep disturbances, insomnia and strong fluctuations in mood and irritability. Naturally, with a new baby, sleep may be hard to get and the normal highs and lows that come from such a monumental life change are to be expected. Think of the hormone adjustments that the body is going through and how that can cause a great deal of upset in the new mother. Just as the hormones ran rampant in the first trimester, the body now has to adjust itself because it is suddenly no longer pregnant.

It takes time for hormones to settle down and for the new mother to get acclimated to the changes both internal – such as no longer carrying a child – and external, like the home invasion that is a new baby in his nursery. First time mothers are especially vulnerable not only because of bodily changes, but also because of the newfound responsibilities of caring for an infant. Again, a supportive family and partner are pivotal in helping the new mother to adjust to this life-altering experience.

Since baby blues are so common in the majority of women, this period of adjustment from hospital to home can't really be considered a full-blown depression. However, if symptoms linger and, unfortunately, become worse, then we're looking at a more serious condition.

If a mother finds that things aren't getting any better even after a routine is established, post-partum depression might be to blame. This condition affects 10-20 percent of mothers and normally develops within the first two to three months after giving birth.

The symptoms for full blown post-partum depression are more profound than after-birth baby blues. They include persistent insomnia and sleep disturbances, lack of bonding with the infant, poor personal care, crying, unrelenting fatigue, suicidal thoughts and even thoughts of harming the baby. Feelings of inadequacy often develop along with guilt – the two feed off of one another in a terrible cycle. Noticeable changes in appetite, either not wanting to eat or overeating can also be part of this condition.

Post-partum depression is a disorder that may follow undiagnosed or improperly treated prenatal depression, which lingers and worsens after birth. In the initial days following birth, it can be difficult for anyone to differentiate between what is normal baby blues and what could be post-partum depression. Having a supportive family that is watchful and aware of what the new mother is going through can help determine if the mother's behavior seems erratic or if she is in distress. Keeping in contact with your medical provider is particularly important after birth.

These symptoms can still be present up to a year following birth, but the earlier it is diagnosed and treated, the more likely a positive and healthy outcome for mother and child...

It is important to note that an even more serious mental illness can ensue following the first two to four weeks after delivery. Post-partum psychosis is an illness that affects one to two women out of 1000, and it can present itself even a year after delivery.

The major symptoms of this depression include auditory hallucinations, delusions, which often involve the baby. Visual hallucinations can also be present. Homicidal and suicidal thoughts are also associated with this disorder. Paranoia, anger, hopelessness and mania are also common. [4]As you can see, this disorder is most serious and needs to be treated without delay. This is not something that can be overcome without help. If you suffer these symptoms or if you know someone who is acting oddly, listen to your gut and get help. It could save lives.

Women whose families have bipolar disease are at greater risk in developing post-partum psychosis. Those afflicted with this disorder have a five percent chance of committing suicide and a four percent chance of committing infanticide. Medical intervention is an absolute necessity to help both mother and child.

After this introduction into the different kinds of depression that can occur during and following pregnancy, it is appropriate to discuss the many treatments and tips that can relieve symptoms and return the mother to homeostasis as quickly as possible. That will allow her to enjoy her baby and her new life as a mother.

Although living with depression is an enormous challenge, there are a wide variety of treatments available that have shown success in treating depression. Now we'll look at some good examples of treatments that are available.

---

[4]Identifying and treating Maternal depression: strategIes & Considerations for Health plans
nIHCM foundation Issue BrIef June 2010

Tips

1. Antidepressants

As we have seen from the previous examples of depression, whether it is prenatal or post-partum, life can be disrupted and the mother can be overwhelmed. Fortunately, there are treatments that can help.

Let's focus for a moment on the number one treatment chosen by doctors for women suffering from moderate to severe post-partum depression. Of the treatments of choice indicated by OB-GYN providers, antidepressants ranked number one and were favored by 96 percent of doctors surveyed. [5]

The most commonly used medications are Selective Serotonin Reuptake Inhibitors or SSRIs. If a woman suffers from prenatal depression, the risks of using antidepressants must be considered. It is crucial that the doctor evaluate the mother's previous history of depression and the current symptoms during pregnancy in order to determine whether or not antidepressants should be prescribed.

The Food and Drug Association has issued an advisory on the risks involved with use of antidepressants during pregnancy. Further, the FDA has warned providers that they should inform their patients about specific risks of taking

---

[5] Dietz PM, Williams SB, Callaghan WM, Bachman DJ, Whitlock EP and Hornbrook MC. Clinically Identified Maternal Depression Before, During and After Pregnancies Ending in Live Births. American Journal of Psychiatry, 2007; 164(10):1515-20.

certain antidepressants while pregnant. [6] Significant risk to the unborn baby are also of great concern when prescribing antidepressants during pregnancy. That said, inconsistencies are present in determining those risks, and the risks for harm caused by the depression needs to be weighed against the risk of taking medication.

Other options for women experiencing depression during pregnancy are available that do not include pharmacotherapy, which will be discussed a bit later.

However, when it comes to post-partum depression, antidepressants have been proven to be highly effective and they could be the best course of action for you. Breast-feeding mothers often worry about the effect antidepressants will have on their baby, but according to research, there is minimal risk for the infant – which means that the mother can heal without more fear or guilt. Yet, there have been no studies about long-term effects on the child, and doctors are advised to keep a close eye on the baby, checking in often during antidepressant treatment. [7]

Mothers are advised to evaluate the baby's behavior prior to treatment and watch for any changes such as sedation, irritability or agitation once treatment has begun. Mothers also

---

[6] University of Illinois, Chicago Perinatal Mental Health Project. Information for Clinicians on Antidepressants During Pregnancy and Breast Feeding – June 2009. Available at:
http://www.psych.uic.edu/research/perinatalmentalhealth/pdf/Medicatio n_Chart_June_2009.pdf Accessed 1/8/10.
[7] http://www.webmd.com/baby/pregnancy-and-antidepressants

can monitor their babies for any of the signs that the antidepressants are having a negative impact on the infant.

Overall, the use of antidepressants can greatly alleviate a mother's depression if the mother faithfully takes the medication and follows her health provider's advice. In fact, the outcome can be downright joyful, because mother and baby can bond the way they were meant to.. Naturally, in more severe depression with the presence of psychosis, treatment can take longer, but staying the course should be favored over abandoning treatment.

In any situation involving pharmacotherapy, a period of trial and error can occur while the proper medication and dosage are determined. Sometimes the antidepressant is the right one, but there needs to be a decrease or increase in the amount taken per day. Occasionally, antidepressants can cause other side effects, like nausea, or they will work more efficiently when taken with a meal; factors like these should be thoroughly considered. As always, the mother should communicate with her health provider on a regular basis for optimal treatment to be attained. If something doesn't feel right, she shouldn't "just ignore it" – a few extra visits to the doctor is nothing compared to a lifetime struggling with depression.

2. Psychotherapy

When given the choice of antidepressant therapy or psychotherapy, most pregnant and/or breastfeeding women normally opt for psychotherapy. In the case of mild to moderate depression, being able to sit down and discuss issues with a licensed psychotherapist is an excellent and viable alternative to medication and doesn't present the risk to either mother or baby. However, the combination of psychotherapy, together with medication, is the gold standard of treatment for depression.

Psychotherapy has many avenues when it comes to this kind of treatment. Interpersonal therapy, cognitive, group and family therapy are options within the counseling framework. Interpersonal therapy is known to be efficacious in as little as six to 10 sessions. [8] It has been found that interpersonal therapy in many cases can be just as effective as pharmacotherapy – which speaks strongly to the powers of the mind and the importance of emotional health.

In treating depression during and after pregnancy, clinicians have found that partners and other family members can also end up depressed. Interpersonal relationships have a tendency to suffer when a family member is down for an extended period. This is particularly true during the period of pregnancy, when the family as a whole can become subdued

---

[8] Thurgood S, 2009

and depressed.. While everyone might try to be supportive and helpful, if they too are depressed and unhappy, their efforts, no matter how earnest, can sadly fall short, compounding the issue.

Family therapy has been instrumental in helping each member discuss how they feel and talk out their problems. With an expert clinician such as a psychologist or social worker, problems can be addressed and solved using techniques that will best help the individuals and the family as a whole.

As mentioned earlier, psychotherapy has many options from which to choose. Let's look at a few of those options now.

Interpersonal Therapy or IPT, briefly discussed already, is a form of therapy that quickly addresses symptoms of underlying depression as they relate to relationships, crises, loss and changes in one's life.

Cognitive Behavioral Therapy or CBT teaches coping skills and augments the person's natural coping mechanisms in order to combat and to ease stress. It uses techniques to train thoughts, perceptions and reactions so that a person does not become overwhelmed within any given situation.

Dialectical Behavioral Therapy, or DBT, is a useful therapy that teaches particular techniques that help regulate emotions and distress reactions. We tend to run into emotional potholes when under stress. By learning ways to avoid those potholes, we have more control over our lives and stress does not become overwhelming.

Psychodynamic psychotherapy studies the pattern and history of subconscious thoughts. Through this understanding, clinicians can teach new coping and avoidance mechanisms that foster negativity.

Eye Movement and Desensitization and Reprocessing Therapy or EMDR, encourages positive thoughts while discounting and avoiding negative thoughts. Positive thinking does work, but when we're under stress, we have the tendency to fall into negativity.

Solution-Focused Brief Psychotherapy is a form of therapy that addresses positive traits and augments those traits in order to bring about a positive change. We all have that ability, but we can easily lose sight of that when under pressure. This technique affirms we can have control.

Group Therapy is a wonderful form of therapy that can quickly dispel the notion that we are alone. By talking to other people suffering from the same problems and going through similar situations, isolation, a major stressor in depression, is subdued quickly. People engaged in group therapy can learn from others how to cope and to find new solutions to problems.

Couples Therapy, as its name suggests, is valuable in helping a couple to remain open, intimate and loving even though monumental changes such as pregnancy are present. This therapy can help renew a relationship and remind the partners of why they came together in the first place.

Psychotherapy does present a myriad of options for those suffering from depression. Used alone or with pharmacotherapy, it has been found to be effective in the treatment of depression.

As we continue with treatment options, let's look at another way depressive new mothers or mothers-to-be can overcome their illness.

3. Massage Therapy

There are amazing treatments that can be used for depression during and after pregnancy that are natural, non-toxic and quite beneficial to both mother and child. One such treatment is massage therapy.

Pregnancy massage is inexpensive and quite effective in helping the expectant mother to relax and find peace. Using massage techniques helps to lower stress hormones, such as cortisol that can be detrimental to our health, especially during pregnancy.

Pregnancy massage may mediate its benefit through the vagal activity response, which acts to lower the heart rate, lower cortisol levels and provide soothing relaxation that benefits the mother and child. The vagus nerve is one part of the cranial nerves and is responsible for autonomic responses such as breathing and heart rate. It is located in the brainstem. Massage can increase this nerve's activation and reduce overall anxiety.

Having a partner do the massage has also been found to be very beneficial – imagine the closeness an expectant mother would feel to know that her baby is within her womb while her partner's loving, gentle touch soothes without. When done properly, pregnancy massage can diminish depression and give an overall sense of well-being to the expectant mother. Studies have also indicated that babies grow better in utero and bone development is much more positive following massage – bone development that pregnant women can feel when her baby starts to give those soccer-worthy kicks!

Even partners that give the massage have found that they too experience a sense of well-being as the power of touch connects them with their partner and the life they have created together. It is recommended, though, that a person learn the right way to massage the pressure points from a medical provider.

It is also found that this kind of massage improves communication between partners, eases fear and anxiety and gives a greater sense of control during the various stages of pregnancy. Bonding between partners during pregnancy can have a positive effect that lasts a lifetime and sets the tone for a loving, happy home in which couples can bring up their child.

Considering all the expenses of pregnancy, this is a very inexpensive and positive option that can help guard against depression and stress. Friends or relatives of an expectant mother who don't know quite what to get her for the shower gift could even pitch in and get her a gift certificate for professional pregnancy massage. Having a positive experience during and after pregnancy is the goal.

Next, we're going to look at an interesting form of treatment for depression

4. Bright Light Therapy

Most of us have heard of seasonal depression that sets in during the fall and is brought about by the lack of sunlight. This disorder is widely found in the agricultural community. Bright light therapy has been an amazing tool that helps those suffering seasonal depression to feel more positive during the long, dark days of winter.

Bright Light Therapy has also been useful for women who choose not to go through antidepressant therapy, especially if they are breastfeeding. It is a safe and highly recommended alternative. [9]

Overall, this form of therapy is inexpensive and has far less risk than medication. Additionally, treatments can be given at home. This is advantageous because treatment is readily available and there is no need to pay for a babysitter while the mother undergoes therapy.

Bright Light Therapy utilizes either a bright light or red light normally considered morning light. Women who used this form of therapy showed a 49 percent improvement rate in their depression baseline scale. [10]

As with any therapy, it is important to be consistent and to go through regular treatments even if symptoms don't subside at first – so while Bright Light Treatment can be highly

---

[9] Corral et al. Arch Women's Mental Health, 2007, 10:221
[10] Crowley et al. Journal of Physiological Anthropology, 2012, 31:15

effective, it is not a first course of action. Fighting depression can take some time. Being judicious about staying with the treatment regimen would be most helpful.

Bright Light Therapy can be considered a brief vacation, similar to spending some time at the beach soaking up the sun (but without the sand in your suit). Keeping positive thoughts in conjunction with this therapy will help those suffering from depression to return to normal more quickly.

5. Acupuncture

This form of therapy has been around for thousands of years and has made its way to the West. Although we mainly associate acupuncture with pain management and healing therapy, it is also associated with the treatment of depression because it promotes overall well-being and health.

The Chinese developed acupuncture and found that it stabilized energy flow and either directed or redirected the flow for the benefit of individual maladies. No less a medical authority than the Mayo Clinic has even recognized the benefits resulting from acupuncture.

Extremely thin needles are inserted just under the skin and can stimulate the nerves and encourage the body's own painkilling chemicals to achieve desired results. This also works for depression and can help the body to balance itself without the intervention and risk of medications.

A recent study indicated that inserting an acupuncture needle under the skin and applying a small current brought about the same effects as Prozac, a medication used for the treatment of depression.[11]

With concerns of side effects that accompany medications, there are added benefits for choosing acupuncture to fight depression. Of the many side effects of antidepressants, one

------

[11] http://www.scientificamerican.com/article/can-acupuncture-treat-depression/*Journal of Alternative and Complementary Medicine Fall 2013*

includes a decrease in libido. That might not seem like such a big deal right away during pregnancy or the first few months with a newborn, but physical intimacy is an important part of relationships, and a prolonged lack of sex between a couple can leave lasting damage. Acupuncture does not bring about those or other side effects and in reality can help the body to regain its normal energy.

The positive response from depression sufferers has been astounding. Pregnant women suffering from depression that underwent active acupuncture or SPEC showed remarkable improvement. Research showed that 69 percent of pregnant women displayed positive results from this therapy. Those numbers equate to other forms of treatment, and the risks are minimal to both mother and child. [12]

Encouraging numbers were also seen in especially high-risk patients – those most profoundly affected by their depression – and proved to be beneficial in lowering the risk for more serious post-partum depression. Consider the saying that begins, "An ounce of prevention..."

Finding an acupuncture provider isn't difficult. Chiropractors and holistic medical providers often offer acupuncture treatments and at a reasonable cost. Using acupuncture therapy is a positive step in the overall battle against depression.

---

[12] Manber et al. Journal of Affective Disorders, 2004, 83:89

6. Exercise

We often overlook the powerful impact of exercise in our lives, even though it is regarded as therapeutic and beneficial. In fact, with our busy and wired lifestyles, exercise is often disregarded, the first thing we sacrifice when we just don't have enough time. We can make countless excuses for not exercising because we're too busy. We lack motivation or we start a regimen only to quit after a week before reaping any rewards.

Exercise is very important in our lives and that is especially true for pregnant women and new mothers, but did you know it's also a valuable treatment for depression? Over the past 50 years, society has become less mobile, more electronically connected. Instead of walking to the mailbox to mail a letter, we sit at the computer and send an email.

Our sedentary lifestyles have caused a chain reaction in our bodies that slows the metabolism, weakens our immune system and often leads to depression. Exercise is a key component to physical and mental health. It gets the chemicals in our bodies charged and as we breathe deeper and our heart rates climb, we alleviate stress and tension as well as depression.

Sedentary lifestyles add stressors of their own resulting in physical, emotional and mental fatigue. By exercising regularly, positive chemicals are released in our brains that ease stress, and help us to sleep better. The results of exercise produce a positive attitude, critical in fighting depression.

Other benefits to exercising while pregnant help the mother during labor. Regular exercise helps promote essential muscle tone. Even after birth, an exercise routine helps a mother lose that extra baby weight , those pesky pounds that stick around after the baby has been birthed and whose presence – which keep women from fitting into those jeans they loved pre-baby – can be depressive. A new mother absolutely can regain her vitality. We often hear people say they're too tired to exercise, yet, exercise is the best way to fight fatigue and regain strength. [13]

Exercising daily is inexpensive – try absolutely free, if you already have some walking or running shoes and a park nearby – and a most invaluable weapon in fighting depression and keeping a positive outlook. It can diminish overall health risks, and can be sound and effective treatment for depression. Of course, it's always a good idea to check with your medical provider before starting an exercise program. With proper guidance, a personalized program can be adopted that will improve health, beat back depression and even add years to your life.

Exercise II

Sometimes women claim that they get enough exercise just doing housework such as vacuuming, mopping floors and

---

[13] LeCheminant et al. Scand J Med Sci Sports. 24:414

making beds or doing laundry. Studies have shown however, that these tasks can actually lead to depression.[14]

You might be surprised to learn that fact. Studies have indicated that involuntary work such as household tasks, adult or child care actually add stress to our lives – certainly anyone, male or female, who juggles daily home upkeep with children and work knows that the struggle is real - which in turn fosters depressing feelings.

Depression can make a person feel they're losing control over their lives. A new baby and a tiring new routine of child care can exacerbate this sense that we are not in control. Exercise on the other hand not only is a positive choice that is beneficial, but it trains the brain and emotions to realize we are in control of our lives and we can take positive steps in helping ourselves to achieve a proper balance.

Simple and low impact exercises like walking, stretching, and even Tai-Chi and Yoga have been instrumental in prenatal and post-partum depression and something than can be done throughout our lives in just minutes per day. [15] We'll look at a couple of those exercises more in depth a bit later.

With newfound balance, depression lessens and we feel more confident on many levels. We know we need to eat, to sleep and to even play. Yet, frequently we forget we do need to exercise. So be kind to yourself and get moving! Just see how quickly your life will improve!

---

[14] Dimissie el al. Journal of Women's Health, 2011, 20:1025
[15] 1744-3881/$ e see front matter 2012 Elsevier Ltd. All rights reserved. http://dx.doi.org/10.1016/j.ctcp.2012.10.001

7. Breastfeeding

It's been known for some time that breastfeeding has positive health benefits for both mother and child. Of the many benefits, breastfeeding can help with post-partum depression. This is due to the fact that the hormones involved, specifically oxytocin and prolactin are known to produce anti-anxiety and antidepressant effects on the mother, while producing healthy results in the child. Such benefits include a boost to the infant's immune system because of the nutrients found in breast milk. [16]

Further, a special bonding takes place between mother and child, giving both a strong sense of security and satisfaction, that indescribable peace and happiness that you see on a radiant new mother's face. Breastfeeding mothers also achieve easier weight loss after pregnancy because the very act of feeding a child from your own breasts burns tons of calories. Getting rid of the baby weight then gives the mother a huge boost of self-esteem.

Additionally, protective aspects are also involved. Breastfeeding helps to regulate a mother's sleep-wake cycle. Getting enough rest post-partum gives the mother a better feeling of self. She is more productive and less likely to be overrun by stressors that can lead to depression. A well-rested mother is capable of more attentive interaction with her child so that both can enjoy their special time together.

---

[16] Borra et al. Maternal Child Health Journal, 2014

Studies have shown this protective effect to be more pronounced in women who planned to breastfeed while pregnant and carried through with breastfeeding after delivery. While some women planned to breastfeed during pregnancy and found for some reason that they were unable to do so, a study found they were at much higher risk for developing depression. [17]

Women who actually desired to breastfeed and were incapable of it can develop profound feelings of inadequacy, which may result in depression. If a woman was already depressed, this can make matters worse.

A strong support system within the family and from the medical community is essential in helping the mother understand that her inability to breastfeed does not make her a bad mother and that she can still have a very positive and profound impact on her child, especially during feeding time. She must also understand that she is not inflicting any harm on her child due to bottle feeding. The input from a mother who, like her, could not breastfeed although she wanted to, but is nonetheless a successful and happy parent, can make all the difference.

The mother's post-delivery life can be very complicated. By the very nature of the large changes in her life, depression can result. Although the positive emotional aspects of breastfeeding may not be available to every woman, other

---

[17] Figuieredo et al. Journal of Pediatrics 2012 4:332

positive treatments are available that can make this time very special. By realizing that each mother is a unique and special person, whether she breastfeeds or not, is something that a supportive family can instill in the new mother.

After all, our feeling of well-being and self-esteem are greatly impacted by the people around us. Keeping positive and going forward with a healthy and positive attitude will make this new experience a wonderful and memorable time.

8. Skin-to-Skin Contact

Immediately after a baby is born, it is highly recommended that the baby be given to the mother for skin-to-skin contact or SSC. This pivotal contact, the first of many occasions when the mother and baby will feel their warm breath upon each other, is important for many reasons. It allows the baby and mother to bond with each other. The baby is also exposed to its mother's bacteria and helps foster the infant's immune system. This is much more beneficial to the baby and its digestive system than bacteria found in incubators.

Emotional and psychological benefits are also experienced. In fact, studies have shown a remarkable decrease in post-partum depression when mothers and infants have SSC. Mothers who have six hours of SSC per day, particularly in the first week after giving birth and then at least two hours per day until the end of the first month, reported far less depressive symptoms than mothers who did not engage in SSC. [18]

If you think about it, that's quite a significant statistic and it's achieved without medication – it is literally just the mother holding her baby! At home, this is as simple as napping on the couch together, which also follows the old advice that you "sleep when the baby sleeps."

How is this result attained? You'll remember we discussed the benefits of oxytocin earlier in our tips. Apparently, SSC

---

[18] Bigelow et al. J. Obstet Gynecol Neonatal Nurse 2012 3:369

increases oxytocin in the mother and gives her a feeling of empowerment, thereby warding off depressive symptoms. (Another interesting fact about oxytocin? It is the chemical associated with falling in love!)

Also noted benefits of SSC are a decrease of both physiological and emotional stress in both mother and child. With that reduced stress, both sleep better, interact more positively and for longer periods of time. That added interaction is also a positive attribute that staves off depression.

Overall, SSC is a remarkable treatment for depression and its benefits help mother and child to have a close, loving relationship and establish a bond that will last a lifetime. The positive health aspects are also an added bonus.

SSC is an easy way to fight depression. It is something that is so positive and healthy that it should be considered by every woman, depressed or not. Even partners can join in SSC and form truly remarkable bonds with the child, an impregnable family unit that can withstand any future hardships.

Knowing more about SSC and other non-toxic treatments helps the mother to know that there is indeed help for depression and that can ease fears and anxieties so often accompanied with pregnancy and post-partum life. By using positive means to overcome negative feelings, the body can regulate itself and foster good health.

9. Transcranial Magnetic Stimulation

An interesting and innovative treatment to fight depression is found in repetitive transcranial magnetic stimulation or rTMS. Perhaps you've heard about electroconvulsive therapy to treat profound depression. Well, rTMS works in a similar way, however it is not as aggressive and is safe. It can be used in the comfort of your home.

Those suffering from depression can use this handheld device. It comes with a headband that secures two conducting sponges and electrodes in place at the sideburn level of the head. By running a small stimulating current through the electrodes, the brain is gently stimulated. This is not painful and has been proven very effective in treating post-partum depression.

The stimulation produces serotonin and other neurochemicals that aid in regulating the body and emotions that can get out of sync due to depression, insomnia and anxiety. Even people suffering from chronic pain and diseases like fibromyalgia have found relief using rTMS.

It is suggested that this treatment be used for 20 minutes, two times per day. Benefits are seen almost immediately. One of the advantages of this system is that a person can regulate the amount of stimulation administered to the brain. If the first settings don't result in a decrease of symptoms after two weeks, it is suggested that the person raise the settings on the device.

This treatment is not very expensive. Devices can be purchased for approximately $599-$699 or, perhaps more cost-effective, can be rented for $199. With the general cost of medications adding up over time, this device's "up front" pricetag could be cost effective in the treatment of post-partum depression without any of the side effects.

Studies have shown that women who suffered from depression and use rTMS regularly for 20 sessions had lower scores on the depressive scale.[19]

Certainly this therapy has many pluses and is making inroads in the fight of depression and is viewed by many psychiatrists as the best choice of treatment without pharmacotherapy.

---

[19] Myczkowski et al. Neuropsychiatric Disease and Treatment 2012, 8:491

10. Hormone Therapy

After a woman gives birth, a decrease in estrogen occurs. This can cause depression to set in. During pregnancy, the body had an abundance of hormones crashing about, creating all sorts of changes, and with the advent of birth, the hormones level off or drop just like estrogen.

Estrogen by its very nature modulates neuronal systems and when its presence is lessened in the body that can be a major contributor to post-partum depression. Experimental therapy is being used to elevate the presence of estrogen in post-partum women who suffer from depression.

This treatment requires the monitoring of estrogen levels, normally using blood samples for the tests. A doctor can evaluate the test results and administer estrogen in doses that would help an individual patient. Each woman is different and must be evaluated as such.

The normal administration of this estrogen treatment is sublingual – meaning it is applied under the tongue – and can have immediate impact. In a study where 23 women had post-partum depression and presented with low serum estradiol levels, (estrogen), a sublingual dose of estrogen was administered. Estradiol acts as an antidepressant in the body normally and by augmenting it in women suffering depression, a positive impact is seen. A noticeable and rapid improvement was noted in their depressive symptoms. [20]

---

[20] http://europepmc.org/abstract/MED/11411813

The good news for breastfeeding women is that taking an estrogen supplement does not appear to harm the infant.

Although this treatment is not generally considered expensive, costs may vary because of duration and frequency of treatment. As with any drug, there are side effects to consider. Some of those side effects can include headache, weight gain, nausea, fluid retention and a tendency toward uterine fibroids, but this is considered rare. Uterine cancer can develop with the use of estrogen with prolonged use, so caution and vigilance should be practiced throughout treatment

When deciding on using this or any other drug treatment, a thorough discussion should take place before proceeding . Only a doctor can help determine whether or not this treatment will work for a particular situation, but it's encouraging to know that this option is available.

11. Yoga/Tai Chi

As mentioned earlier, Yoga and Tai Chi can be a wonderful form of exercise that reduces stress and brings about a general sense of well-being. Let's look at them more in depth now and see how they can help alleviate depression during and after pregnancy.

Both Yoga and Tai Chi help in moderating sleep disturbances, helping an individual get sufficient rest, a factor which has proven to reduce the risk of depression. The body thrives on exercise and these two low impact exercises can be done by almost everyone.

In fact, it has been shown that using both yoga and Tai chi together bring about a very positive energy and chemicals in the body that foster emotional and physical homeostasis. These exercises can be done throughout pregnancy, but some yoga positions are more difficult in the third trimester due to weight gain and the baby's growth making it hard for the expectant mother.

An interesting study was conducted on 92 pregnant women who used yoga and Tai chi. Sleep disturbances were resolved as well as anxiety and depression. Tai chi had a very positive effect in the third trimester, a good point to note since yoga at that stage might be impossible. [21] That's wonderful news for pregnant women, but what about women depressed post-partum?

---

[21] Field et al. Complementary Therapies in Clinical Practice 2013, 19:6

There is good news for women suffering from post-partum depression who use yoga. In 57 depressed post-partum women who received eight weeks of yoga intervention therapy, they displayed significant improvement in anxiety, depression and sleep disorders as opposed to their counterparts who did not follow the yoga regimen. These women experienced a much greater sense of well-being and felt more in control of their lives. Positive changes experienced by those women resulted in happier and healthier lives. [22]

Yoga and Tai chi are very inexpensive. Tai chi requires no special equipment to buy or clothes. Wear anything comfortable. As for yoga, a simple yoga mat can be found at very economical prices. Free videos and how-tos are available online – all you have to do is use your search engine. The only real investment is your time, about 20-30 minutes per day – perhaps while the baby is napping or when the partner is home to watch the infant.

It has also been found that women who take time out from child care and spend 30 minutes per day exercising, were not only less likely to suffer depression, but appreciated their child all the more when they returned.

New mothers can be inundated with all their new responsibilities and can often feel guilty leaving their infants, even if only briefly. Yet without a time out now and then, a mother can be overwhelmed and to a crying baby change and may escalate into anger or aggression.

---

[22] http://ir.ciowo.edu/etd/4825

Yoga and Tai chi are not only good stress relievers, but they also teach how to calm the mind and body and bring them under control. No one can stay on a treadmill of duty without a break, a little "me time"; neglecting one's need for a rest from responsibility can be a set-up for something will snapping eventually. That's why exercise and time out are so vital in the life of the mother.

12. Omega-3 – Fatty Acids

With a growing baby on board, the expectant mother may be depleted of essential omega-3 fatty acids. As the baby grows in utero, its needs increase in order to flourish properly. Doctors believe these needs are the reason that the omega-3 fatty acids levels dip in the mother. Omega-3 fatty acids are a key component in fighting depression and like estrogen, when their levels diminish, a woman is more likely to become depressed.[23]

By supplementing omega-3 fatty acids during pregnancy, a woman experiences more resiliency and as the levels normalize, depressive symptoms go down. For instance, in one double-blind study, 36 women were randomly selected. Of those 36 women, 24 actually completed the study. Some women received omega-3 fatty acids supplements and some placebos. Those women who received the omega-3 supplements showed lower numbers on the depressive scale as opposed to the women who received a placebo. [24]

The fetuses experienced no harm from the omega-3 fatty acids supplements.

It is interesting to note that omega-3 levels can still be low after delivery and therefore supplementing those levels for a time after birth could possibly help in quelling post-partum

---

[23] http://www.ncbi.nlm.nih.gov/pmc/articles/PMC3046737/
[24] http://www.ncbi.nlm.nih.gov/pubmed/18370571

depression. Scientists do feel that more studies need to be conducted to further understand and analyze the effects that take place with the administration of supplements. Great progress is being made though and it should also be noted that this is an effective means of fighting mild to moderate depression.

Statistics differed, however, in women who had previously suffered depression and then had symptoms return post-partum. Studies involving these women were discontinued because their symptoms exacerbated. [25]

Nevertheless, in women who had not had previous histories of depression, the omega-3 supplements appeared to work rather well in lowering depressive symptoms. If you happen to suffer from prenatal or post-partum depression, talk to your doctor about checking your omega-3 levels and discussing the possibility of taking supplements.

For breastfeeding mothers, there is good news. This treatment does not seem to have ill effects on infants.

---

[25] http://www.ncbi.nlm.nih.gov/pubmed/20099994

13. Folate

Having enough folate in our diet is absolutely essential to keep our bodies balanced. This is especially true in pregnant women. Even before getting pregnant, women need to make sure they're getting enough folic acid in their diets to lower the risks of birth defects. Unfortunately, lower levels of folate in pregnant women, particularly in the first month can lead to severe birth defects like neural tube defects or NTDs. Conditions like spina bifida, where the spinal cord doesn't close, can present problems for the child their entire lives. Other defects associated with low folate can be life-threatening to the infant. Where the mother is concerned, lower or falling levels of folate can indeed cause depression.[26]

Normally, the levels of folate deplete in a woman approximately five months into the pregnancy and can continue to dip well past delivery. Lower levels of folate can lead to depression, and this is particularly true in women who are of a genetic predisposition that causes lower folic acid levels. Groups with Celtic, Northern Chinese and other ethnic groups who live in countries where folate-enriched diets are not found can be particularly susceptible to naturally lower folic acid levels.

Other factors should also be considered because they have a profound impact on folate levels. For instance, diabetes,

---

[26] http://womensmentalhealth.org/posts/folic-acid-and-risk-of-perinatal-depression-is-there-an-association/

smoking, obesity, antiepileptic medications and the ingestion of sulfonamides seem to be antagonistic toward folate.

Supplements are available and even can be found over-the-counter. Eating a diet that contains cereal, rice, pasta and other grain products along with lean meat, poultry, tomato juice, broccoli and other vegetables can, when eaten regularly, boost folate levels.

Sometimes that is not enough and a prescribed supplement is in order. If you have concerns that you're not getting the right amount of folate or if you are experiencing depression, ask your doctor to check your folate levels just to make sure everything is fine. Even though you may be taking prenatal vitamins with folate, if you are in a particular risk group or you have a genetic predisposition that lends itself to folate deficiency, you still might need even more folate supplementation not only to protect against depression but also birth defects.

Be sure to consult your doctor and see if you are indeed at risk. A diet rich in folate will not only help to keep depression at bay, but helps ensure a healthy baby.

14. St. John's Wort

For those seeking natural herbal remedies, St. John's Wort has been known to alleviate depression and can be very effective. Many midwives actually prescribe this herbal remedy for women suffering from post-partum depression. Yet, no one should rush into adding this supplement without proper investigation.

First, St. John's Wort has been known to have severe side effects when used with other medications. The use of oral contraceptives and other medications in conjunction with St. John's Wort can bring about serious side effects. If you are suffering from post-partum depression, it is very important to ask your doctor if this treatment is right for you. Be sure to tell your doctor all the medications you are currently taking to make sure that a drug interaction will not occur.

This remedy really only addresses mild to moderate depression. Studies are inconclusive as to safety using this herb when breastfeeding. While some information suggests that the baby receives minimal amounts of the herb in breast milk, there is not enough documented evidence to suggest it would be safe. Again, please consult your doctor.

Use of St. John's Wort during pregnancy should only result after checking with a doctor, because although this herb is readily available and is found on the shelves in most health food stores, people assume that it might be safe. The labels can be misleading or lack sufficient warnings about possible side effects and drug interaction.

Still, if you do not plan to breastfeed, St. John's Wort can be a very good remedy for mild to moderate post-partum depression. As with any substance, it is best to get all the facts before deciding if this particular remedy will work safely.

There have been some studies of lactating, post-partum depressed women that suggests that St. John's Wort can be quite therapeutic in handling depression with minimal effects on the infant. Both mother and infant were observed and found there were no serious signs of problems with the regular use of this herb. [27]

Proponents of St. John's Wort feel that this herb is a wonderful treatment for depression and is preferred over regular pharmacotherapy. A woman's case history should be thoroughly investigated to make sure there are no known contraindication when using St. John's Wort.

---

[27] http://www.drugs.com/breastfeeding/st-john-s-wort.html

15. S-adenosylmethionine

S-adenosylmethionine or SAM-e is a naturally occurring compound in the body. It has a pertinent role in keeping the body stabilized. You might recall seeing the synthesized SAM-e on shelves in health food stores. This compound has been used to treat depression for some time.

While there have been studies done on SAM-e, many were flawed and proper conclusions about its efficacy could not be determined. Some medical experts, however, feel that SAM-e work as well as tricyclic antidepressants and perhaps are safer since the compound already exists within the body. By supplementing patients with lower levels of SAM-e, it is felt that mild to moderate depression can be relieved, welcome news to pregnant or post-partum mothers

Preferred doses that brought about a lowering of depressive symptoms are normally within the 400-1600mg range in a daily dose. As with other types of antidepressants, some experimentation might be necessary to find the right level. There are side effects with SAM-e such as restlessness and anxiety.[28]

SAM-e are compounds that help metabolism, neurotransmitters, receptor activity and membrane fluidity. Lower levels of these compounds can be indicative of depression.

---

[28] http://www.webmd.com/vitamins-and-supplements/lifestyle-guide-11/supplement-guide-sam-e

Post-partum mothers involved in a placebo study presented lower depressive characteristics in women treated with SAM-e. Due to its natural presence in the body, many health professionals think that this might be a safe remedy for those suffering from depression. By raising the SAM-e levels within the body, it works on a natural level with minimal risks or side effects. That is very attractive to many women whose bodies are going through such enormous changes. .

Other positive aspects of SAM-e are its protective liver function characteristics. This quality can be very helpful to treat bile flow obstruction during pregnancy. [29]

SAM-e supplements have only been available in the United States since 1999, but have been around in Europe for some time and have been thoroughly studied. Doctors here in the US have found that SAM-e supplements can work in half the time it takes other antidepressants to work.[30]

In the case of post-partum women, that quick response would be beneficial in getting the mother stabilized so she can focus on enjoying her new baby and all the milestones to come. It's been often found that the drawn out treatments can have a negative impact on those suffering from depression because they desperately want relief in a hurry. This dietary supplement seems to answer their needs.

---

[29] Freeman, Journal of Affective Medicine 2009 112:1
[30] http://www.psychiatrictimes.com/articles/investigating-sam-e-depression

16. Homeopathic Remedies

The body is very powerful and remarkably has the power to heal itself. Homeopathic healing providers commonly use natural substances in minute quantities and administer them to the sick patient to address specific maladies. Those small doses would make a healthy person sick. The practice was first established in Germany during the 18th century and has become widespread. Even Medical Doctors are using this approach in curing their patients. The general idea of homeopathy is that symptoms either physical or emotional, like those experienced during depression are normal reactions. The body is giving signs that something is out of alignment.

Homeopathic remedies can be wonderful. They're natural and inexpensive and normally have few side effects. Natural remedies are highly preferred to medications, particularly those used in the treatment of depression in pregnant and post-partum women. We've already discussed some natural remedies, but there are others we should explore as well.

Sepia is used for women who don't feel attached to the babies or families and have other depressive symptoms. Sepia originates in the ink sac of a cuttlefish. Some homeopathic providers feel it's quite efficacious in the treatment of depression. Sepia is used when women feel isolated from their families and do not understand why. These women take proper care of their babies and families, but they do so grudgingly or view it as a duty, while lacking energy and happiness. The use of sepia, which can be used long term post-partum is a common homeopathic remedy.[31]

Ignatia is another powerful homeopathic remedy that has proven effective in post-partum depression or when people are grieving or have experienced some sort of loss. Ignatia comes from the St. Ignatius Bean, which is a rather tall woody shrub. This remedy is quite good for handling women that overact to situations and are high strung. If a woman is cranky or easily agitated, Ignatia eases those symptoms.

Natrum muriaticum is another homeopathic remedy that works well with people who are depressed, but don't like to admit it. They have a strong sense of duty or obligation to perform up to specific standards. Thanks to the pressure caused by our super-connected world, where we all know each other's business and where mothers can use social media to brag about themselves or shame others, new mothers can fall into that category and suppress their emotions until things catch up to them. Too many bottled up emotions can result in a volcanic reaction that would be detrimental to the family and the newborn baby. Natrum muriaticum levels them off, relieves stress and symptoms of anxiety and depression.[32]

While homeopathic remedies are not for everyone, they're worth looking into if you're interested in the natural approach

---

[31]
http://drfeder.com/index.php?page=articles&action=viewArticle&articleID=224

[32] http://www.britishhomeopathic.org/bha-charity/how-we-can-help/conditions-a-z/beating-the-blues/

to fighting depression. Homeopathic providers are quite prevalent as society has learned that a natural approach to medicine is very positive.

17. Aroma Therapy

We all know what a positive effect a pleasant smell has on our moods. The smell of something delicious baking in the oven can raise our spirits, reminding us of home or our own mother and put us into a good mood. Some doctors believe that aroma therapy can be a good treatment for depression. So let's investigate this remarkable remedy.

By using essential oils and in conjunction with massage therapy, a post-partum woman can find relief from depression. Sometimes, the basics in treatment, like using touch therapy and massage work just as well, and often better than pharmacotherapy. Just as touching is so essential for a newborn baby to feel secure and loved, it is also important for adults as well.

Mothers, particularly just after delivery, expend a lot of love and might not get that in return from a partner due to a variety of reasons. Focused on everyone else, the new mother forgets about her needs and depression can develop.

With aromatherapy and massage, essential oils are used on the skin, creating positive physical and emotional reactions. Imagine lying down, feeling the tension melt out of your body as a beautiful, soothing scent envelopes you in peace. Just the sheer relaxation can produce positive flow of serotonin and other crucial chemicals that allow depression to lift.

By using lavender and neroli oils, it's been found to have an uplifting effect on mood and sense of well-being. The aroma relieves anxiety and if massage is used with those oils, the patient relaxes and outlook improves. The simplistic nature of this remedy makes it quite appealing, while these particular oils have a sedative effect to them.

In studies done of mothers who went through aromatherapy and massage, they exhibited far lower numbers on the baby blues scale. [33]

It was also discovered mothers that participated in this therapy had lower numbers across the board especially in hostility, anger, anxiety and depression, emotions that can run rampant if left unchecked in women caring for newborns

Most studies done on aromatherapy were not conducted on lactating women. Therefore, it has not been adequately determined if this kind of therapy is safe for breastfed infants. Also, not all essential oils are safe during pregnancy. It is important to check if the aromatherapy oil is recommended during pregnancy, and also it is a good idea to do a small patch test first to make sure that the oil will not cause any allergy. Yet, it does provide a great and pleasing alternative for all those suffering from depression.

---

[33] Imura et al. Journal of Midwifery Women's Health, 2006,51:e21

18. Hypnosis

Hypnotherapy is a treatment that zeroes in on subconscious thoughts and retrains the brain to have positive thoughts. This is done by creating a focal point and addressing negativity at the subconscious level. The goal of hypnosis is to root out the negative thoughts and perceptions and replace them with positive ones.

Generally, our consciousness takes up only 10 percent of our mind. Hypnosis addresses the entire mind and the whole person. Treatment is administered accordingly. We might be surprised to find out how much residual and undiscovered anger, resentment, guilt, doubt and other negative feelings lie trapped in the subconscious. [34]

All the negativity can lead to depression, if it's not addressed properly. Many of us use coping mechanisms that resemble sweeping dust under the rug rather than meeting the issues head on. Hypnosis works in the opposite way by sweeping up all that negativity and discarding so that it will hopefully not return. During a hypnotic state, unpleasant memories or emotional upsets can be identified and addressed without stressing the patient and then subsequently removed.

In the process the mind is trained to be more positive, to conquer fears and deal with anger and all the other emotions

---

[34] http://web.wellness-institute.org/blog/bid/266024/Five-Ways-to-Treat-Depression-with-Hypnotherapy

that can fester beneath the surface. Clinical hypnotherapy goes right to the heart of the matter by addressing the underlying reasons for depression.

Unlike medications that tend to numb the mind and ease some symptoms, hypnosis goes straight to the cause. Hypnotists know how to get to the deepest recesses of the mind to loosen disturbing and repetitive thoughts that are counter-productive.

All that negativity just doesn't program us to respond in certain ways, but it also has a profound influence on our entire body. Negativity can be the root cause of many illnesses and unless confronted and dealt with, will eventually manifest in serious bodily harm. It's as though through our subconscious we're punishing ourselves.

Once those specific traumas are dealt with, the patient regains self-esteem. Guilt, anger and resentment can no longer be used as a weapon against the mind and body.

Now that you have learned a little bit about how hypnotherapy works, it's easy to see that this is an ideal therapy for both pregnant and post-partum women who are depressed, as it's non-invasive and has been recommended for mild to moderate depression. It can also be very beneficial to new mothers and obviously does not harm the child.

19. Meditation

We have a great deal of noise in our lives, from phones, radios and television. There is not enough quiet time in our lives. As such, we easily become stressed out and we start to become anxious, depressed and angry.

Western researchers have found that by adopting meditation, the symptoms of depression are lessened. To do that, we have to learn to turn off all the outside stimuli and "just be" for a while. By envisioning positive places in our minds that we're seen or would like to visit, we can calm our heart rates, lower anxiety and feel more like ourselves again.

With a crying baby who might have colic or teething, nerves can quickly become frayed, especially if the mother is not getting needed rest. In a way, the practice of meditation can bring about that rest in only minutes per day.

By concentrating on breathing slow, deep breaths, by letting our jaw drop open a bit and closing our eyes on the world for a few minutes, we can find a wonderful vacation spot within our minds that calms our distress and relaxes the body. When we're stressed our muscles tighten and that can lead to headaches, knots and general discomfort, which only heightens our negativity. When we interact with others, negativity can snowball and be contagious. Before we know it, everyone is upset. Depression follows. [35]

---

[35] http://www.everydayhealth.com/depression/treating/alternative-treatments.aspx

Besides deep breathing, meditation teaches us to relax each muscle group, from our toes to our heads. As we focus on relaxing our toes and moving up our body, depression is relieved incrementally. By the time we reach the top of our heads, our bodies should be well relaxed and we can regain our composure.

Meditation also works well for women in labor and the relaxation techniques that accompany meditation can be very good for the baby.

An infant knows instinctively when a mother is upset, even if she doesn't say a word. The infant can feel the muscle tension in its mother and it's been reported that babies then tense themselves. The tension leads to crying and thus a vicious circle begins. That's not positive for the child nor the post-partum depressed mother.

With practice, meditation can be most effective in handling depression. We just have to be willing to be religious about setting time aside for meditation.

Meditation might not be the perfect solution for all women or for more serious depression, but it's an alternative therapy that has only positive side effects. It certainly is worth trying if you suffer from mild to moderate depression, be it prenatal or post-partum.

20. Doulas and Home Visitors

A doula is a woman who is trained to assist women in childbirth to care for newborns and their mothers. They have a wealth of information about childbirth, newborn care and everything in between that new mothers need to know.

Doulas are particularly useful in the first crazy days after bringing home the baby. She can smooth things over, help with feeding, diapering and ease the mother and the rest of the family into the changes a new baby brings to the family.

A doula can counsel and support a mother. Often just having a doula in the home helps the mother to relax, because just knowing there is someone present who has seen it all and done it all can help to ease depression. Grandparents don't often live in the same city and that makes getting supportive help at home next to impossible.

However, a doula is the perfect answer. Mothers can nap without fear of something happening to the baby. Fathers don't have to worry about cooking meals or doing laundry. The family can then enjoy this very exciting time.

It has been found that doulas and home visitors are a very positive form of treatment not only for women suffering post-partum depression, but all new mothers who need someone to lean on.

Doulas have been so instrumental in helping families through the transition of a new baby that women who did have mild to moderate depression quickly got through it. A new mother can be taught by the doula to focus on what's important, to remind the mother to take care of herself. It's almost like having a nanny for adults.

With love and care, doulas can establish a feeling of control in the mother and the mother can learn valuable coping skills to help in the days ahead. Sometimes the learning curve is so great with new mothers that they can easily become depressed at the enormity of the situation and with all the newfound responsibilities.

By learning a new routine of how best to handle certain situations, the mother gets a tremendous education and develops positive coping mechanisms that will see her through her new experiences long after the doula leaves.

Sounds great, doesn't it?

Before hiring a post-partum doula, be sure to check her references and get to know the candidates so that you find a doula who will be the perfect match for your family. [36]

---

[36] http://www.babycenter.com/0_how-a-postpartum-doula-can-help_1199772.bc

21. Healthy Life Style Choices

We've talked about exercise in the fight against depression and how important it is to achieve the proper balance in our lives. It is also important to focus on diet, not only during pregnancy but after delivery. New schedules and demands brought about by a new baby in the house can lead to irregular eating habits. Eating too little or too much can lead to problems. Avoid junk food that is high in sugar and has little nutritional value. If you put good things in, you will get a good performance from your body in return, and that is something the entire family needs when there is a new baby in the home.

Without proper, balanced nutrition, our bodies don't get the necessary fuels they need to keep healthy, to ward off depression and disease. So we need to look at positive steps in prenatal and post-partum diets to make sure the proper nutrients are included.

Keeping away from sugary foods or fast foods will help stabilize blood sugar, mood and provide the proper nutrition to meet with the demands of pregnancy and post-partum childcare. Most people don't realize what a drain both conditions can be. With busy schedules and/or a lack of interest in eating, we tend to grab a bite here or there while the baby is napping and don't consider the consequences of what we're eating.

It's been mentioned earlier that our bodies are made up of chemicals. When we have an improper diet, those important chemicals can be thrown off. Eating enough protein, good carbohydrates, fruits and vegetables are a great help in keeping both mind and body fit.

Proper nutrition also helps breastfeeding mothers to keep up with the new demands. While losing baby weight is a priority for most women, cutting back on calories can be the first choice. However, this may not be the best option. More calories are required when breastfeeding. Consuming the right calories in the proper amount several times a day will keep the body and mind balanced. New mothers can ask their doctors what the appropriate caloric intake will be for their height and weight with breastfeeding factored in.

A person sleeps better, thinks better and has more energy with the correct diet. We have seen what a lack of rest, and a disturbance in the body's chemicals can do when it comes to depression.

Therefore, it's important to plan out your meals so that they are nutritious and satisfying. You might set aside time at the beginning of every week to create healthy meal plans for the next seven days. Also make sure to throw in a small treat once in a while. Naturally, eating heavy deserts everyday won't improve your waistline after delivery, but having that mini-cupcake or cookie every once in a while is good for you.

Think of your diet plan as everything in moderation. Moderation is key not only to losing weight but also in having enough fuel to keep going and to keep your emotions in check.

If you are breastfeeding, you should be <u>consuming</u> an extra 500 calories per day. The total calorie intake should be somewhere between 2300 - 2500 calories per day. If you are not breastfeeding or pregnant, the daily calorie count should be 1800-2000 per day. [37]

By checking your calorie count and maintaining proper nutrition, risk for depression and ill-health will be lower. Skipping meals to lose weight will only work against you.

Sure, your want to lose that baby weight , but do it sensibly. Be patient and follow a healthy regimen and you'll succeed in attaining your goals.

---

[37] http://kellymom.com/nutrition/mothers-diet/mom-calories-fluids/

22. Avoid Isolation

Sometimes we can get so caught up with our schedules that we have a tendency to isolate ourselves from friends and families. Being a new mother, this can be especially true. New mothers tend not to go out as much and if they do, it's normally for doctor visits for the baby and shopping for necessities.

Yes, there are a million things to do with a new baby, from diapers, to laundry, feeding times and taking care of the rest of the family. That's all necessary and important. However, it's just as important to take care of you!

If you limit your activities to just the essential trips to the store or doctor and you spend most of your time at home, feelings of isolation can ensue quickly. That's not healthy for anyone, and that's really true for new mothers.

Isolation can lead to depression, a very tough depression. When we don't go out often, even just to walk, to see friends or go to a movie, a sense of not wanting to go out at all can develop. This is an unhealthy mindset that will only have detrimental effects.

Be sure to keep up with friends and family. Go out on a regular basis. Having a scheduled date night also helps to keep a healthy relationship with partners. You've heard the adage about all work and no play...it is absolutely essential to go out and have some fun that doesn't involve the baby. Get a reliable babysitter or a doula and you won't have any worries about spending an evening out at least once per week.

Our relationships shouldn't be put on hold because of new family responsibilities. On the contrary, they should be encouraged.

Having a strong support group around you will help with depression and anxiety. Learn to lean on people when you need them. Sometimes people hate to volunteer to help because they don't want to risk offending someone. Often, people are just waiting to be asked. [38]

We're not sentenced to hard time when a baby arrives, but sometimes it may feel like that. Be innovative and return to outside activities, bowling, cards, and date night, whatever it is. You might have to get creative about how you make the time, and things certainly won't be as carefree as they were before the baby's arrival, but you don't have to feel guilty about keeping up on your hobbies, interests and social life.

A happy mother will have a happy baby. Partners, too, can step up and make sure that they are doing all they can in the home with child care and housekeeping and in ensuring that the new mom gets out on a regular basis.

You'll be surprised how you both feel when you get that all-important time out. Moods will elevate and you'll look forward to spending time with your wonderful new baby.

Life is like a garden. It needs to be watered frequently to help it thrive. You don't have to go to extravagances. Find

---

[38] http://mayoclinic.org/diseases-conditions/postpartum-depression/basics/lifestyle-home-remedies/con-20029130

something simple you enjoy doing and then do it. Don't make excuses. Just like feeding times are fairly well set, time out should also be scheduled.

Be sure not to chuck out romance with the dirty diapers. Get back into the swing and remember that your partner has needs too. With everyone getting proper attention and time out, life can be beautiful and certainly less overwhelming.

23. Make Time for Yourself.

We touched briefly on this point earlier, but let's investigate some positive ways of looking after yourself. If you enjoy reading books or have special TV programs you love to watch, remember to schedule them into your busy day. While interrupting feeding time or distracting yourself with TV while trying to nurse or to feed your baby is not a good way to bond with your child, you can record your favorite shows and watch them during "Me" time. Read that book while the baby is napping and catch up with your email and the news online.

Everyone needs a bit of time away to recharge and regroup. It's a key component to keeping a positive mental outlook. Further, it reduces stress and anxiety.

Another aspect to consider is proper grooming. Mothers, especially new mothers, are very judicious about making sure their babies are bathed, hair brushed, and dressed in the latest fashions. They spend a lot of time making sure everything is right for their child. However, all too often mothers neglect their own appearance.

You'll see new mothers running to the store in lounge pants, hair askew, no make-up and they don't seem to care. Yet, their babies are all dressed up. Eventually, this will go against the mother, as a less fixed-up appearance becomes a habit. There is absolutely nothing wrong with having to run to the store in yoga pants and a ponytail, but an entire year without getting dressed up or having a reason to put on make-up can cause the mom to develop negative feelings toward herself and her attitude, and her self-esteem will plummet. [39]

New mothers can think they're too busy to get their hair colored, nails done or to spend some time getting a massage. When their appearance starts to go downhill, partners start to look at them differently. All sorts of emotions and attitudes come into play and not in a positive way.

We all have the need to look our best. It doesn't mean we have to be designer dressed, but it does mean we should take time to make sure that we are the best we can be, not just for others, but more important, for ourselves.

Depression can bring about a sense of no value and this really grows when we look in the mirror and see a reflection of how we look – or see something worse. Weight gain is common and depression more common in mothers who let themselves go.

Just as mothers learn to reschedule their lives to accommodate their newborn, mothers can also figure out a specific time of day and a certain day of the week for personal time. It's not that hard. Sure, it might take some ingenuity, but if you consider the negative avalanche of emotions that develop by not taking time to take care of yourself, you find that it's well worth the effort.

You don't have to go overboard and become a demanding princess, but do pamper yourself a bit. You'll feel so much

---

[39] ibid

better and so will those around you. When we let our appearance go, we actually build walls around us that keep people away. However, when we take the time to look and feel our best, we become a positive magnet, a person that will attract the right kind of attention. [40]

So don't drive people away by not taking care of yourself. Yes, it's admirable to take care of others, but some personal pampering will keep joy in your life. Go get that manicure; we bet you any money that accompanying hand massage will feel so good you might find yourself biting back tears.

---

[40] http://www.parents.com/blogs/great-expectations/tag/postpartum/

24. Don't Expect Too Much of Yourself

One quick way to develop or add to depression is expecting too much of yourself. It is very common for new mothers to take on the world and want to be the best mom, wife, cook, and problem solver in the world. Social media has been found to make this problem even worse, as women post statuses and photos that make it appear they are doing it all – but they are actually just posting one moment out of hundreds each day, and the enormous majority aren't so picturesque.

Too often women set goals for themselves that no one person, let alone ten, could possibly attain. Once you hit your stride in pregnancy or after delivery, it may seem that you are capable of doing remarkable things, to be the be-all and the end-all of everything. You can set goals for what you expect of yourself or what you perceive others expect of you.

Having unrealistic expectations is setting yourself up for a nasty fall and depression. Those unrealistic goals may seem noble and make you think you are capable of doing remarkable things. For a time, that may be true, but like a tire that gets worn, all too often it will blow out or become flat.

Today, women are not only juggling childcare, and marriage but also a job at the same time. That's quite a load for anyone. We fail to realize our bodies have limitations and sooner or later, they will start to break down. Our emotions, too, can only take so much without getting a respite.

Women are especially prone to depression who have the mindset that they can be supermoms and super-wives all the while keeping a full-time job. The impossible nature of our goals will eventually hit us right between the eyes.

Therefore, setting reasonable and attainable goals is crucial in avoiding depression and physical or emotional breakdown.

Realizing you are only human and can only do so much will go a long way in living a healthy life. Babies can sense strain and tension from their parents and those around them. By having unrealistic goals and pushing ourselves to remain at a certain level produces a tremendous amount of stress. Babies will react and as mentioned previously, a horrible vicious cycle starts.

If we realize that by setting goals too high, we're paving the way for failure, it's easier to find reasonable solutions to be all you can be without pushing yourself to be Wonder Woman!

Don't be afraid to ask for help when you need. Be honest with yourself about what you really can and cannot do. Your family doesn't want a super hero that's all stressed out and depressed. They want you to be you....happy, healthy and engaged!

Realizing perfectionism is impossible, you'll find happiness is much easier to achieve.

Another good point to mention is that as you adjust to your new life with your baby, try to limit visitors. You won't feel the panic that sets about whether or not the house is presentable. Just remember, the house may not be in perfect shape, but if it's picked up and reasonably clean, you're ahead of the game.

There is no sense killing yourself trying to be perfect!

25. Talk to Other Mothers

We mentioned that being isolated is unhealthy for depressed mothers. By not having someone around to listen to us and to tell us that we're not alone, can be a very scary situation. Isolation can lead to a sense of helplessness and things may seem hopeless.

That's why pregnant and post-partum women should find other women in the same situation. Talking out problems, discussing fears and finding answers for things from those more experienced, can certainly help in eliminating depression.

There is a therapeutic quality that is found in groups. As women discuss their personal problems in a group setting, the weight of the problem lifts. A problem shared lifts the burden from the person going through the difficulty. Nothing is more reassuring to a depressed mother to share a problem and have someone tell them that they went through the same thing and how they resolved it. [41]

Others might chime in with their take on things and what helped them. All of sudden you're not alone and your spirits will elevate. If we don't share problems they tend to grow on us and we feel that they are insurmountable when that might not be the case. The whole process of sharing reduces anxiety and stress.

---

[41] http://www.postpartumprogress.com/ppd-support-groups-in-the-u-s-canada

It's even possible, especially under group chats, to find something funny about the circumstances. Laughter is one of the best means of fighting depression. It releases positive chemicals in our bodies and before we know it, we're feeling better.

Although things can appear frightening and disconcerting when you're depressed, listen to a friend whose been there and survived. That can show us that our problems are not uncommon and that there are solutions.

Commiserating with those in the same situations bolsters our self-esteem. We become part of something bigger than ourselves. We begin to look past ourselves, our problems and focus on someone else. Even the act of listening to someone else is a positive step that leads to reaching out and sharing problems.

A special bond can form in these groups and they can become extended families for those suffering from depression. Having a group available also helps when partners are tied up with their schedules and we need answers to questions sooner rather than later.

Strong support systems are extremely valuable in fighting depression. They're like having a safety net beneath us, there to catch us if we fall. There are other advantages to a support group. Frequently, depressed moms don't want to share certain things with their partners and they keep it bottled up for fear their partner will make a judgment call. However, in a support group, everyone is on equal footing and that helps us feel we can open up and discuss what is bothering us.

When we verbalize our problems to others who are sympathetic to our needs, we actually hear the problem for the first time. Just hearing the problem in our own words, we might discover that it's not that big a problem. Let's face it. During and after pregnancy, our hormones make us react to things in a much different and bigger way than we normally would. Hearing the actual problem frees the mind from all the inner dialogue that skews our perceptions. Sharing the problem with like-minded people immediately cuts the problem in half.

So why not join a group that will be supportive to your needs? It can make a big difference in how we face the challenges of depression.

26. Get Extra Rest

As soon as the baby goes down for a nap, it might seem like a great time to catch up on housework or laundry. Yet, you really should think about getting extra rest. Your body is still recovering from the pregnancy. It's been said that sleep is the universal panacea and that's true.

Studies have shown that if a women gets plenty of rest and doesn't push herself, her coping skills and her resiliency in handling day-to-day stress are much better. Lying down while the baby sleeps is a great way to recharge your batteries. Remember, fatigue can lead to depression or exacerbate a depressive bout. You might not think you're tired enough for a nap, but you'll be surprised that you can doze off quickly.[42]

Don't let the long list of things you have to do keep you from resting. The chores will keep for a time. Be good to yourself and get the rest you need.

By regularly taking naps, you allow your mind and body to heal and to fortify you for the times when you can't nap.

Certainly, if you don't take advantage of naptime, you will regret it down the road. As mentioned previously, a body can only stand so much. This isn't a question of being lazy and avoiding things by napping. Rather it's a healing time that will make coping easier. A time will come when you won't need as

---

[42] http://www.keeperofthehome.org/2012/02/postpartum-rest-and-recovery-tips-from-a-mama-who-learned-the-hard-way.html

much rest, but during and immediately following pregnancy, you will do wonders for your overall health.

The baby has a set sleep schedule and it's highly recommended for mothers to do the same. Each day at the same time you know it's your time to nap. Don't cheat. Take the time you need. You'll find depression will improve and so will your energy.

You can't do it all and rest. So ask the family to chip in and help with various chores around the house. Of course, that only works if you take your hands off the reins and allow someone to help you. It doesn't mean you're weak, lazy or a bad mother. It simply means you're tired and you need your rest.

Too often mothers make the mistake of hitting the ground running after delivery and they don't realize just what the body has gone through. Nevertheless the body and emotions have a way of letting you know sooner or later that you've done too much.

The most effective way to recover from this life changing experience is to rest and cut yourself some slack. Your baby needs to rest in order to grow. You need rest in order to heal.

Don't overdo and you'll find that life isn't as daunting as it appears.

27. Keep a Journal

Talking things out in group is a marvelous therapy, but you might find that you don't always want to share certain things. Try keeping a journal. You can record your innermost feelings, and write about what is going on with you on a much more personal basis. There is no fear of judgment. You're free to openly let out your feelings. [43]

Journaling is really beneficial to pregnant and post-partum depressed women. By faithfully recording your thoughts and feelings, you have a daily account of how things are going. You can read what you've written a month or two ago and see how far you've come. The highs and lows of each day will be there for you. Problems can be jotted down as well as solutions.

When we look at things too closely, we fail to see the bigger picture. For instance, today might be a rough day and you record that. Tomorrow just might be better and you record that. In time, you'll have a better understanding of things and see it in perspective.

You will be able to spot trends in the down times. The cause of those bad times might become more evident or you can see a pattern take shape and learn how avoid the things that caused the problem.

---

[43] http://www.postpartum-living.com/journal-therapy.html

Keeping a journal is inexpensive and it's a pro-active solution. You can actually take charge of your own treatment. Evaluating your progress and the daily events can be a fabulous history for you years down the road. Milestones such as a baby's first laugh, smile or word can all be recorded for posterity.

It's important to journal about all the things in your life so that when compiled you can see that not everything is negative. Happy and beautiful things are happening all the time. It's not always tough and emotional. Sure, there are clouds, but the sun does shine through throughout the day.

Many doctors encourage their patients to keep journals, whether they are using pharmacotherapy or psychotherapy. Doctors may want to read the journals to see what things are really bothering you and to observe your progress with medications.

Journaling helps to appreciate the small things in life. Added together they comprise stepping stones to happiness.

Keeping the journal fair and balanced as best you can, will ensure an accurate picture of your life and what is really going on A catharsis takes place when we journal and we get rid of the things that are bothering us. Once they're written down, move on and go through the day.

Set aside a time to journal when you won't be interrupted and you can focus on writing. Be honest and let the words flow. Maintain your journal on a daily basis. Set a specific period of time that you will keep the journal. You'll be amazed as you go back to see how positive things have become.

Think of the journal as a before, during and after project. It's a great therapy with no harmful side effects, costs or unpleasantness.

28. Keeping a Routine

As discussed, babies have their routines and so should mothers. By keeping your daily routine, you can defend yourself against depression. Shower, brush your teeth, do your hair and your daily chores at the same time every day. You'll notice babies do better and feel more secure with a daily routine. So will you.

Routines can keep us on track and moving forward. They're like keeping a checklist. We have some many things within our routine and we can mentally tick them off as we go. Too often when depression sets in, we let our routines slide. That's the worst thing we can do.

Time seems to drag or it can get away from us and we find we're behind in what we need to do, which can be depressing. Routines have a way of motivating us and when we get through them all at the end of the day, time seems to have flown. We have a sense of accomplishment.[44]

Depression tends to lure people from the norm of daily life. It throws supposed roadblocks in our way and a small bump in the day can be perceived as in insurmountable mountain.

We need to distinguish the good routines from the bad. Removing the bad routines like smoking so many cigarettes a day or eating junk food at a particular time can and should be

---

[44]http://stayontop.org/2012/12/14/dont-break-your-routines/

discontinued. Fostering and keeping good routines can instill a good sense of self and allow us to move forward.

Depression can keep us stationary in a very uncomfortable pit. Positive routines maintain order in our lives and block disorder that sets in with depression.

Routines don't have to be rigid. We can loosen the routine a bit, but we should never break the routine. Consistency is key and it's important to know that. For instance, if you drive a certain way everyday as part of your routine, then try another way, but don't drop the routine.

If you shower after breakfast, try showering before, but don't give it up either. Mixing things up can help avoid getting bored. However, whatever you do, keep doing it. Be sure though not to add too many things to your routine particularly after delivery. Ease into changes, but go through your regular routine without fail.

It won't take long before you realize that you're happier with the routine. Completing your daily routine without cheating is a great accomplishment. It's a positive step and allows you to keep control.

29. Reduce Stress

Don't allow yourself to be overwhelmed by too many obligations or social events. Keep things to a minimum in order to avoid stress. Having people over or agreeing to take part in too many activities can stress you out too much leaving you cranky and fatigued.

It's important to do what you can, as much as you can without pushing yourself. If you find you can't get everything done, don't worry. Pick it up later.

Enlisting your family's help will reduce anxiety and a lot more can be accomplished. Share the load and don't try to carry it all by yourself. As we've seen, that's impossible to do for long.

Once you realize your life has changed and accept the fact that things will never be the same, it will be easier to work through depression. You have moved on to a new stage in life. Some things might have to change. That isn't necessarily a bad thing because with your new life there are exciting times ahead. There's no sense getting too stressed and fatigued because you'll miss the most rewarding time in your life. [45]

So breathe deeply and let stress go. Friends and family will understand. You can learn to have fun and relax. Jettison the things that aren't working or the social obligations, at least for a time, so that you can overcome your depression.

_____

[45] http://www.marasworld.com/natural-postpartum-depression-remedies/

People don't realize that they add stress to new mothers by insisting that the mothers join them in this or that function. It doesn't mean you have to become reclusive, it does mean you should become selective in what you agree to do.

Don't let people send you on a guilt trip for not participating in certain things. Guilt is a very good friend to depression and life will quickly seem miserable if you give in to it.

A good suggestion is to make two lists. One list if for the things that cause stress in your life and the other is for the things that reduce it. See what works and see what doesn't. Take control of your life so you don't get run over by all the rush of activities. Get your family involved. They might be able to find ways they can help eliminate stress. They will feel better because they're helping you and you'll feel better because it's one less thing to worry about in your life.

30. Ask for and Accept Help from Family and Friends

We've touched upon this all important therapy, but now we'll take a closer look. Sometimes, when we're overwhelmed or suffering from depression, we wonder why people don't give us any help.

To us, it's obvious that we need help. Yet, to others, that might not be as obvious. This is really true for women who have been the dynamo in the family, capable of handling all sorts of things and juggling tremendous loads. Families tend to believe that this kind of person is totally in charge and everything is fine. After all, it always has been.

Too often women that are this capable become very adept at hiding their fatigue and weaknesses, not wanting others to see them. In reality, that's very harmful. So, when things get rough and depression has a tight grip, the woman and the family are surprised when she hits a virtual brick wall.

As much as we love our partners and families, we can often be baffled as to why they don't pick up on what's wrong. For some reason, we're astounded because they just don't "know." We think they're psychic or something. When our partners and families fail to respond, this can bolster depression and leave us feeling all the more alone.[46]

---

[46] http://www.postpartumprogress.com/what-to-do-when-youre-too-afraid-to-ask-for-ppd-help

Since most people aren't psychic and are caught up in their own schedules and things, it is best for the woman in need to sit down and talk with them. Tell your family what is going on. Chances are they won't know it. They might have seen signs or symptoms, but they need to hear what's actually going on. It's not that they're resistant to helping out. It's more that they don't have a clue.

So don't be afraid to vocalize that you need help. It doesn't make you less of a person and it isn't a burden to your family. Families must work together to keep the family afloat and healthy. If we think about it, we don't want our families to hide things from us when they're in need.

Then we shouldn't keep things from them. When one family member is hurting, the whole family hurts. Depression may hit a pregnant or post-partum woman the hardest, but her family also goes through the disorder.

Rather than letting things blow up and get out of control, be honest. Tell your family what you're going through and what you need them to do. Don't assume they know. By being frank and asking for help, you give them the chance to be charitable and to forget about themselves for a while. That's healthy for them and for you.

Asking for help is only painful if you allow it to be. Take a deep breath and let your family and friends know exactly where you are and what you need them to do. Working together for the common good and for the health of the family is a positive thing. It teaches children to know that everyone has limits. Everyone needs help. The whole process of sharing your problems allows the family to grow and to come together, rather than growing apart. Silence does drive wedges into relationships.

31. Encouraging is Key

We all need encouragement in our lives and when things get rough, we need it all the more. It's good to know that we are on the right path, that we're making the right choices and doing positive things. Encouragement is a wonderful way to get beyond depression.

By reading uplifting articles and watching inspirational movies or TV shows, we are encouraged to do better. It's a way of comparing where we are, and where others are. If we find that we're not doing as badly in comparison to other people, we're encouraged to keep trying.

Families can help a great deal in encouraging the depressed woman. By being supportive, she'll know she's needed, and loved. Everyone needs the confirmation in their lives that they make a difference in someone else's life.

Partners can have a great impact in the encouragement process. They can relate stories or find books that offer hope. A pat on the back and telling the depressed woman she's doing a great job is something that should be done with regularity.

Life after delivery is hard and depression makes it harder. Kind words, a gentle touch, cooking a meal or just spending time with the pregnant or post-partum mother can be a fabulous boost to her spirit.

The mother also needs to know that her role is one of the most influential in the world. By her sacrifices and love, she is raising a human being to enter society and to be a positive contributor. That's no small task. So be proud of what you've done and what you continue to do.

Motherhood is a heroic undertaking and not for the faint at heart. It's terribly fulfilling role. Yes, it does have its ups and downs, but it's also a thrilling experience.

Don't allow yourself to be influenced by negative press on your role as a mother. Motherhood should never be discounted. Stay away from the negativity and focus on the positive aspects of your tremendous role.

If that's not always easy, look at the things you achieve daily in your life and your family's. Concentrate on all the positives.

As the days progress, things will become easier and almost second nature. There might be hurdles to jump every now and then, but they'll get easier too. Before long you'll be an expert and wonder why things seemed so overwhelming at first.

Time passes quickly and before you know it, your baby will be heading off to school. With all your patience and good habits you're developing now, you'll be ready for that day and the new challenges ahead.

Depression doesn't have to get in the way of your life. It might slow you down for a time, but it won't defeat you. You are in control.

Keep a positive attitude and be encouraged that you've come a long way. You can also be encouraged that you have developed extraordinary skills that will serve you well throughout your life.

You can control depression by taking positive steps. Seeking out the positive things in life will help you overcome the greatest difficulties. Perhaps none is as challenging as motherhood, but then nothing is as worthwhile.

Be encouraged then and take heart!